Animals and the Environment
Snakes

Cottonmouths

by Linda George

Content Consultant:
Donal M. Boyer
Associate Curator
Reptile Department
San Diego Zoo

C A P S T O N E
H I G H / L O W   B O O K S

C A P S T O N E   P R E S S

818 North Willow Street • Mankato, Minnesota 56001
http://www.capstone-press.com

Library of Congress Cataloging-in-Publication Data
George, Linda.
    Cottonmouths/by Linda George.
        p. cm.--(Animals and the environment)
    Includes bibliographical references (p. 44) and index.
    Summary: Describes the physical characteristics, habitat, and behavior of the poisonous snakes known as water mocassins or cottonmouths.
    ISBN 1-56065-694-8
    1. Agkistrodon piscivorous--Juvenile literature. [1. Water mocassin. 2. Poisonous snakes. 3. Snakes.] I. Title. II. Series: Animals & the environment.
QL666.O69G467   1998
597.96--dc21

                                 97-31672
                                    CIP

Editorial credits:
Editor, Matt Doeden; cover design, Timothy Halldin; illustrations, James Franklin; photo research, Michelle L. Norstad

Photo credits:
Dembinsky Photo Assoc. Inc./Allen Blake Sheldon, 12
Jack Glisson, 32, 34
Bill Love/Blue Chameleon Ventures, 46
Bob Miller, 20
Len Rue Jr., cover, 36
Toops Stock Photos/Connie Toops, 22
Unicorn Stock Photos/Bill McMackins, 11
Visuals Unlimited, 26; Joe McDonald, 4, 6, 15, 16, 19, 28, 39, 40, 43; John D. Cunningham, 25; Joel Arlington, 31

Table of Contents

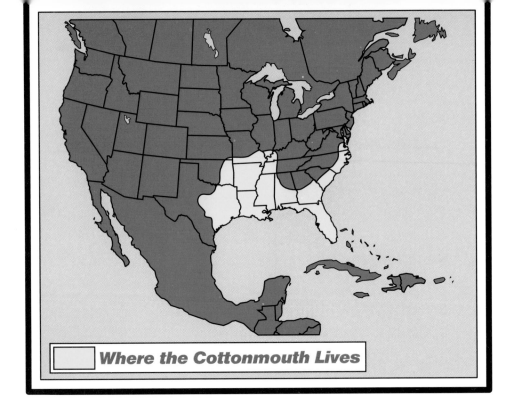

Where the Cottonmouth Lives

Fast Facts about Cottonmouths

Kinds: Cottonmouths are members of the Viperidae family. A family is a group of animals with shared features. People call some snakes in this family pit vipers.

Description: Cottonmouths have flat, triangle-shaped heads. Most cottonmouths are olive or tan. Some are black. Cottonmouths have brown stripes around their bodies. Their undersides are yellow. Cottonmouths may have black or brown markings on their undersides.

Habits: Cottonmouths climb into trees or bushes above slow-moving water. They wait for fish and frogs. When they sense danger, cottonmouths open their mouths wide. They do this to frighten enemies.

Food: Cottonmouths eat mostly fish. They also eat frogs, lizards, rats, and mice.

Mating: Cottonmouths mate in early spring. Female cottonmouths give birth in August or September. They have one to 16 young snakes.

Life span: Cottonmouths live up to 20 years.

Habitat: Cottonmouths live near freshwater bogs. Bogs are muddy, shallow bodies of water. Cottonmouths also live near lakes, streams, and other bodies of water.

Range: Cottonmouths live in the southeastern United States.

Chapter 1

About Cottonmouths

Cottonmouths are members of the Viperidae family. A family is a group of animals with shared features. People call some snakes in this family pit vipers. Pit vipers have loreal pits near their eyes. These pits sense body heat from other animals.

Cottonmouths are named for their white mouths. The insides of their mouths look like cotton. Cottonmouths open their jaws as a

Cottonmouths are named for their white mouths.

warning when they sense danger. People also call cottonmouths water moccasins, gapers, and snap jaws.

Description
Cottonmouths are large snakes. Most adult cottonmouths are about four and one-half feet (1.4 meters) long.

Cottonmouths have flat, triangle-shaped heads. Most cottonmouths are olive or tan. Some are black. Cottonmouths have brown stripes around their bodies. Their undersides are yellow. Cottonmouths may have black or brown markings on their undersides.

Young cottonmouths have brighter skin than adults. The colored bands of young cottonmouths are outlined with white. The tips of their tails are bright yellow. Young cottonmouths look like young copperheads. Copperheads are another kind of pit viper.

Most cottonmouths are olive or tan.

Cottonmouths become darker as they grow older. Old cottonmouths turn dark green or brown. They may lose their stripes and markings. Some become all black.

Where Cottonmouths Live

Cottonmouths live in the southeastern United States. They always live near water. This is because most of their prey lives in water. Prey is an animal hunted by another animal for food.

Cottonmouths spend much of their time hunting for prey that live in the water. Many cottonmouths live near swamps. Some live near slow-moving streams.

Cottonmouth Senses

Cottonmouths sense mainly through smell and taste. They flick their forked tongues out every few seconds to smell and taste the air. Their tongues sample the air around them. Cottonmouths rub their tongues against their

The pupil of a cottonmouth's eye is a thin slit.

Jacobson's organs. The Jacobson's organs are tiny sacs at the top of their mouths. These organs are special taste and odor detectors.

Cottonmouths see better at night than some snakes. The pupil of a cottonmouth's eye is a thin slit, like a cat's. A pupil is the black part of an eyeball that lets in light. Many snakes have round pupils.

Cottonmouths' narrow pupils give them better night vision than many other snakes. The narrow pupils help gather more light. Cottonmouths see about as well as other snakes during the day. They have poor vision from far away. They can see nearby objects best.

Cottonmouths have loreal pits between their eyes and nostrils. The loreal pits help cottonmouths find prey at night. Loreal pits sense body heat. The pits help pit vipers find other animals even when there is little or no light.

Cottonmouths cannot hear because they do not have eardrums. But cottonmouths can feel vibrations in the ground. Vibrations are movements of the ground caused by moving animals. Some scientists think cottonmouths use these vibrations the way other animals use hearing.

Cottonmouths have loreal pits between their eyes and nostrils.

Molting

Like all snakes, cottonmouths molt. Molt means to shed an outer layer of skin. A cottonmouth has several layers of skin. One layer holds the snake's scales. Another gives the cottonmouth its colors. These are not the layers cottonmouths shed. Cottonmouths shed the layer of clear skin that surrounds the scales.

Cottonmouths grow a new layer of outer skin while they molt. The skin over a molting snake's eyes turns white. Soon, the skin begins to peel away from the mouth. The snake wiggles out of the peeling skin. The skin turns inside out. The snake leaves it behind. The snake already has a new layer of outer skin. Cottonmouth colors and markings are especially bright right after the snakes molt.

Cottonmouth colors and markings are especially bright right after the snakes molt.

Chapter 2
Hunting and Defense

Cottonmouths are camouflaged. Camouflage is coloring that makes an animal look like its surroundings. Camouflage helps cottonmouths hunt without being seen.

Cottonmouths can also defend themselves. Cottonmouths warn enemies when they are about to bite. They open their mouths and raise their heads. They do this to frighten away enemies.

Cottonmouths warn enemies when they are about to bite.

Cottonmouth Prey

Cottonmouths eat fish, frogs, turtles, birds, and lizards. They also eat rats and mice. Some even eat young alligators.

Most cottonmouths hunt animals that live in water. Some cottonmouths climb trees near lakes or slow-moving rivers. The cottonmouths hang down from branches above the water. They wait until prey comes near.

Cottonmouths drop into the water when they sense prey. They bite and hold their prey. They inject venom through their fangs. Venom is a poisonous liquid produced by some animals. A fang is a long, sharp tooth. A fang has a hole at the end so venom can pass through it.

Some cottonmouths hide near water to hunt. Camouflage helps cottonmouths remain hidden from prey. Other cottonmouths swim with their heads above the water when they hunt. They bite and hold their prey underwater. Then they carry the prey to land.

Cottonmouths hang from branches above the water.

A cottonmouth swallows prey headfirst.

Swallowing Food

A cottonmouth swallows prey headfirst. It swallows the prey whole. Sometimes the prey is still alive. The bones in a cottonmouth's jaw can open wide. This allows the snake to eat large prey. A cottonmouth often eats animals larger than its own head.

Swallowing takes a long time. A cottonmouth's teeth grasp the head of its prey. The snake uses muscles to pull the animal inside its body. The prey often struggles as it is swallowed.

Cottonmouth Defenses

Cottonmouths are camouflaged. Sometimes people walk near cottonmouths because they cannot see the snakes. Many bites occur when people accidentally step on cottonmouths.

Cottonmouths raise their heads when they are alarmed. They open their mouths wide. They show the white inside their mouths to warn enemies. Cottonmouths will bite people if they sense danger. But they often try to escape instead of biting.

Some cottonmouths move their tails back and forth when enemies come too close. When cottonmouths do this, they are getting ready to bite.

Chapter 3

Cottonmouth Venom

Cottonmouths are known for their deadly venom. They are among the most venomous snakes in North America. Cottonmouth venom can kill a full-grown person.

Cottonmouth Fangs

A cottonmouth's fangs curve back into its mouth. The fangs swing forward when the snake bites. A

A cottonmouth's fangs curve back into its mouth.

cottonmouth must open its mouth wide to bite. The fangs inject venom through small holes.

The cottonmouth's venom makes its victim bleed inside. The victim can bleed for hours after being bitten. The victim may also have difficulty breathing. Venom can also make a victim's heart beat faster.

Venom affects small prey almost right away. It takes longer to work on a large victim like a person.

Cottonmouth Strikes

Unlike many snakes, cottonmouths do not seem to fear humans. Cottonmouths readily strike humans who come too near. Strike means to wound by biting. Many cottonmouths will not use venom on animals they cannot eat. But cottonmouths may use venom if they sense danger.

The skin near a cottonmouth bite swells. Sometimes the swelling keeps blood from reaching a hand or foot. This can paralyze parts

Cottonmouths do not seem to fear humans.

of the hand or foot. Paralyzed means unable to feel or move part of the body. Victims often feel weak, thirsty, or sick. They also have trouble breathing.

Treating Cottonmouth Bites

The victim of a cottonmouth bite must see a doctor right away. A victim may become paralyzed if a doctor does not treat the wound.

Doctors can treat cottonmouth bites with an antivenin. An antivenin is a medicine that reduces the effects of venom. Scientists use the chemicals in snake venom to make antivenin. Most victims must take antivenin in shots.

Taking venom from a cottonmouth is dangerous. Scientists hook a cottonmouth's fangs over the edge of a jar. Venom comes out of the fangs and drips into the jar. Scientists call this milking a snake.

Scientists hook a cottonmouth's fangs over the edge of a jar to take venom.

Chapter 4
Mating

Cottonmouths mate in early spring. Female cottonmouths have one to 16 young in August or September. Cottonmouth young are on their own as soon as they are born.

Mating Rituals

Cottonmouths perform rituals during mating. A ritual is a set of actions that is always performed the same way.

Sometimes male cottonmouths fight for a female. The males fight on land or in the

Cottonmouths mate in early spring.

water. The male that wins the fight may try to approach the female. The snake that loses moves away.

A male cottonmouth approaches a female on land or near the water's edge. The female lets the male line his body up with hers if she wants to mate. The snakes may twist their tails together while they mate. The male cottonmouth moves away after mating. He may try to mate with other female cottonmouths.

Young Cottonmouths

A group of young cottonmouths is called a brood. A female cottonmouth does not stay with her brood. Young cottonmouths know how to care for themselves as soon as they are born. They already know how to hunt prey.

A male cottonmouth moves away after mating.

Young cottonmouths are brightly colored. The tips of their tails are yellow. They use the colored tips to draw prey near.

When prey comes near, the young snakes wave their tails slowly. Some animals may try to eat the cottonmouths' yellow tails.

The cottonmouths attack if the animals are small enough to eat. The young cottonmouths try to escape if the animals are too large.

Young cottonmouths are often too small to stop their prey from running. They may hold on to their prey while the prey tries to escape. The prey usually stops trying to escape after several seconds.

Young cottonmouths have bright yellow tails.

Chapter 6

Cottonmouths and People

Cottonmouth venom can kill people. But cottonmouths also help humans. They eat rats and mice. Rats and mice eat crops. Cottonmouths keep rat and mouse populations from growing too large.

Meeting a Cottonmouth

People should avoid cottonmouths. Their bites are painful and can be deadly.

Cottonmouth bites can be deadly.

Cottonmouths are also hard to see. People should wear boots and loose pants when they are walking in areas where cottonmouths live. Boots and loose pants can keep a cottonmouth's fangs from touching a person's skin.

People walking in areas where cottonmouths live should watch the ground carefully. They should not lift rocks or logs. Cottonmouths often live under these objects.

It is best to stand still if faced with a cottonmouth. Sudden movements can frighten the snake. A cottonmouth needs plenty of room to escape. The best way to escape from a cottonmouth is to back up slowly.

Killing Cottonmouths

Some people hunt and kill cottonmouths. They kill the cottonmouths because the snakes are venomous. But cottonmouths are not in danger of becoming extinct. Extinct means no

Cottonmouths often live under rocks or logs.

longer living anywhere in the world.

Many people have difficulty telling cottonmouths from non-venomous water snakes. People kill water snakes because they think the snakes are cottonmouths.

Scientists who work with snakes can tell cottonmouths from water snakes. They look at the snakes' heads. Cottonmouths have slitted pupils and loreal pits. Water snakes have round pupils and no loreal pits.

Most cottonmouths live in swamps and wetlands where few people live. Most people do not want to build near cottonmouth territory. This keeps people safe from cottonmouths. It also keeps most cottonmouths safe from people.

Most cottonmouths live in swamps and wetlands where few people live.

Head

Tail

Scales

Markings

Words to Know

antivenin (an-ti-VEN-in)—a medicine that reduces the effects of snake poison

brood (BROOD)—a group of young snakes

camouflage (KAM-uh-flahzh)—coloring that makes an animal look like its surroundings

extinct (ek-STINGKT)—no longer living anywhere in the world

fang (FANG)—a long, sharp tooth; venom passes through it

loreal pits (LOR-e-uhl PITS)—small holes between pit vipers' eyes and noses; the pits sense heat

paralyzed (PA-ruh-lized)—unable to move or feel part of the body

prey (PRAY)—an animal hunted by another animal for food

ritual (RICH-oo-uhl)—a set of actions that is always performed the same way

venom (VEN-uhm)—a poison produced by some animals

To Learn More

Ethan, Eric. *Cottonmouths*. Milwaukee: Gareth Stevens, 1995.

Ethan, Eric. *Vipers*. Milwaukee: Gareth Stevens, 1995.

George, Linda. *Copperheads*. Mankato, Minn.: Capstone High/Low Books, 1998.

Stone, Lynn M. *Poison Fangs*. Vero Beach, Fla.: Rourke Press, 1996.

Useful Addresses

Fort Worth Zoo
1989 Colonial Parkway
Fort Worth, TX 76110-6640

Metropolitan Toronto Zoo
West Hill
Box 280
Toronto, ON M1D 4R5
Canada

National Zoological Park
3001 Connecticut Avenue NW
Washington, DC 20008

**Society for the Study of Amphibians
  and Reptiles**
P.O. Box 626
Hays, KS 67601-0626

Internet Sites

Cottonmouth Water Moccasin
http://www.wf.net/~snake/moccasin.htm

Slithering Snakes
http://www2.excite.sfu.ca/pgm/students/alex_reid/
 snakes/MAINPAGE.HTM

The Snake Page
http://www.geocities.com/CapeCanaveral/4538

Western Cottonmouth
http://birch.palni.edu/~drigg/wcotton.htm

Index